SO, YOU FOUND YOURSELF A HUMAN, NOW WHAT?

Charleston, SC
www.PalmettoPublishing.com

So, You Found Yourself a Human, Now What?
Copyright © 2022 by Karin Block

First Edition

Paperback ISBN: 979-8-88590-741-5

So, You Found Yourself a Human, Now What?

HOW TO TRAIN YOUR HUMAN

GINGER BLOCK

with a little help from her human Karin Block

Illustrated by: Kerrie Robertson

DEDICATION

To my humans who were so easy to train, and who continue to treat me like a princess as I deserve. And to all my friends who encouraged me to write this book. I couldn't have done it without you.

TABLE OF CONTENTS

INTRODUCTION

As a puppy, I found myself not one, but four, humans. Even at the young age of eight weeks, I realized the importance of training these humans to take proper care of me. And so began my journey.

Over the years, I have trained my humans to treat me like royalty. They have realized that they are here to serve me and grant me my every wish and desire. Some would call me spoiled, but I believe I deserve this treatment. And I believe you do too! With just a little bit of training, your humans will begin to treat you with the respect and admiration that you deserve.

In order to properly train your human, you must first understand them. Humans are unusual creatures. They come in all shapes, sizes, and abilities. Their two most notable features are their great height and their opposable thumbs. These two features, and their desire to make us happy, are what you will use to train your human.

While humans are typically intelligent and loving creatures they can be easily confused. This characteristic often causes them to believe that they are in charge. This book will show you how to disavow them of this notion.

Let's begin!

TRAINING METHODS

For most lessons, we will employ one of two training methods to teach your humans, the "Annoyance Method" and the "Guilt Method." Each of these methods has been proven effective in a variety of situations. In the pages that follow, you will learn the best times to use each of them as well as how to best apply the method in each training session.

ANNOYANCE METHOD

The best way to teach your human is to employ what I like to call the "Annoyance Method." This method requires you to behave in a manner that your humans consider to be annoying. This is easily done because they are very easily annoyed.

Surprisingly, many behaviors that annoy a human are behaviors that we consider polite communication. While barking at our friends is perfectly acceptable to us, humans do not appreciate being barked at. They also dislike being tripped as they walk, being pawed at while they sit comfortably, and having their ankles nipped at while they walk. You must get to know your particular human and discover for yourself what they find most annoying.

One point to remember is that it is important to vary your annoyance methods from lesson to lesson. By using a variety of methods, you will be able to teach your humans that each annoying behavior of yours means something different. This is important to avoid confusion. Remember humans are easily confused so you must keep it simple in order for them to understand. In the pages that follow, I will suggest methods that have worked for me. You may need to modify these methods according to your humans' individual behaviors.

GUILT METHOD

Another method you will use to train your human is the "Guilt Method." As the name suggests, your human will be made to feel guilty when they do something you don't want them to do. This method is best used when your human is doing something that you find scary or uncomfortable. Humans don't like to see us sad, unhappy, or scared. If we let them know that their behavior is making us feel this way, they will feel guilty. And a human who feels guilty is a human who is easily trained.

BASIC IDEAS YOUR HUMANS MUST GRASP

In order to train your humans, we must first discuss some very basic ideas. Humans really do want to make us happy, but often lack the knowledge to do so. They mean well though and are typically easy to train. By first teaching your humans that you are in a position of authority and that they should listen to you, your life and happiness will almost immediately improve.

WHO IS IN CHARGE, REALLY?

Before we begin truly training our humans, we need to teach them about the proper hierarchy of the household. You see, humans have a bit of a superiority complex and seem to believe they are in charge of things. The truth of the matter is that they are here to serve us, and we are, in fact, in charge of the household. From the moment we wake up in the morning to the time we go to bed, humans' thoughts and actions should be focused on serving us and our desires. The sooner humans realize that they were put on this planet to serve us, the better.

This concept is very difficult for an untrained human to grasp. I suggest using the Annoyance Method here. You must be very annoying each and every time your human acts like they are in charge. Barking loudly usually works because humans do not like to be fussed at. But your particular human might respond better to a different annoying behavior. The important thing to remember is that your human must learn this particularly important lesson before they can be trained further. You must therefore give it all you've got. Bark, run around in circles, nip at their ankles, whatever it takes for them to stop their behavior. Once they stop, they will be ready for the next lesson. Remember you must act quickly though, otherwise they will forget and begin acting superior again.

LISTENING SKILLS

Listening skills are of utmost importance! When we listen to each other, we show that we care about, respect, and love each other. Our humans appreciate it when we listen to them. They enjoy it when we sit, come, and stay when they ask us to. And yet, it is rare when a human naturally listens to us. I have found that listening skills do not come easily to them and they must be trained to respect our authority. This all-important lesson will need to be learned before humans can master any future lessons.

We will use the Annoyance Method to train your humans to listen. If your human is doing something you do not wish them to do, you must annoy them until they realize the errors of their ways. Some humans grasp this lesson much easier than others. Perseverance is key!

A favorite method of mine to annoy my humans is to bark. It is important to let them know they are doing something that displeases you and barking seems to do the trick. For this to work, you must maintain eye contact while you bark. Humans must learn that prolonged eye contact means you are discussing something with them, and they will begin to pay attention to what you have to say. When they have learned to listen, you will be able to train your humans to do anything you want them to do.

LET THE REAL TRAINING BEGIN

Now that your humans understand the true hierarchy of the household and have a basic understanding of the listening skills required to keep you happy, it is time to begin training them to do what you want and need them to do for you. These lessons are arranged in order of importance. However, they can be completed in any order according to your specific needs.

FOOD

The topic of food is one that is very confusing to humans. For reasons unknown to me, humans believe it is wise to limit our food consumption. They are wrong about this and must be taught that we should have an unlimited supply of scrumptious food. It is confusing to me as to why this is a difficult lesson, as they also thrive on three meals a day and snacks. But alas, humans have difficulty grasping several topics that seem simple to us.

MEALS

In order to thrive and be happy, we need at least three meals a day. Sadly, this is one of the more difficult lessons for humans to master. I, myself, spent a good part of 12 years teaching and reteaching this lesson to my humans. Finally, at the age of 12 ½ my humans mastered the concept and I now receive four meals a day (Breakfast, Lunch, Dinner, and Second Dinner). As you can see, perseverance is key. If you don't give up, I have confidence that you can enjoy at least three, and possibly more, meals each and every day.

Teaching your humans the importance of providing you with frequent meals requires you to master the Annoyance Method. You must make them uncomfortable. Humans will do almost anything to continue living in comfort, so this method works nicely.

One thing most humans seem to dislike is falling. I, therefore, recommend tripping them as they walk in the kitchen. Due to humans' great height, this is an easy task for those of us closer to the floor. As they stumble about trying not to fall, humans become more and more desperate. They will do almost anything to discourage us from tripping them. This is when you sit politely and look at where they keep your food. It's always a good idea to reward them by wagging your tail and giving them kisses when they give you something to eat. It is through this method of annoyance followed by positive reinforcement that even the most stubborn human will learn to feed their non-human children more often.

SNACKS

Humans enjoy snack-time. They start their lives eating many snacks throughout the day. As toddlers, they enjoy cereal and crackers during car-rides. Parents are known to coordinate snack deliveries to various sporting activities. Even as adults, humans are known to bring snacks with them when they know they will be away from home for a while and might feel hungry. Why then is it so difficult for humans to understand that we, too, enjoy snack-time? While an answer to this question would be lovely, it is hardly necessary for our purposes. Instead of understanding the why's of your humans' behavior, we must focus on training them to change their behavior to suit our needs.

Ideally, a human could be trained to keep the snacks on the floor within our reach. They could be trained to use those fabulous thumbs of theirs to open our snack bags and just leave the bags scattered around on the floor. Ideally, we would always have an open snack bag nearby. Unfortunately, I have found it exceedingly difficult to train my humans to do this. Humans can be stubborn when it comes to scattering food around the floor. For this reason, I suggest compromising with your humans. Humans are much easier to train if they believe they have a little bit of control over the situation. So, while it is less than ideal, I suggest allowing your humans to believe it's their idea to feed you snacks and treats. If they are allowed to keep the

19

snacks on the kitchen counter or in a cabinet or drawer, they will feel a sense of pride when they see your happy face as they give you a snack. This sense of pride makes them happy, and a happy human is much more likely to want to make you happy again and again.

How do you train them to believe they are in control while simultaneously keeping all the control for yourself? Once again, I recommend the Annoyance Method. Using this method, you can train your humans to give you a treat at regularly scheduled intervals. Some recommended opportunities for snack time are when you come in from outside, when your human is leaving the house, when your human comes back into the house, when your human enters the kitchen, and when your human is getting themselves something to eat. Obviously, there are many, many more opportunities for a snack, but you will have to decide on these times yourself. When would you like a treat?

The method of annoyance that you use will vary from human to human. I have found that tripping my mommy is a method that works quite well but barking incessantly at my daddy is what works for him. Many humans dislike constant barking. This method works well for almost all training needs. If you are persistent with your method, your human will soon be trained to give you a snack every time you ask. Eventually, they will give you something before you begin annoying them to avoid the behavior they are bothered by. When this happens, they will believe it is their idea to feed you to make you happy. Let them believe this as it keeps them happy. A happy human will occasionally give you something to eat even when they haven't been trained to do so at that moment. This behavior must be rewarded with positive reinforcement. Wagging your tail in happiness will make your human wish to repeat this behavior. Soon your human will be taught to open snack bags for you several times throughout the day.

GROOMING

You will soon discover that humans have some absolutely crazy ideas about grooming. Among other things, they enjoy bathing and manicures. Many of us do not. You will need to decide for yourself how often you wish to be bathed and have your nails trimmed and train your humans to behave accordingly.

Sadly, the Annoyance Method does not work as well here. To train your humans to groom you on your terms, I recommend the "Guilt Method."

BATHS

I think the most important thing for humans to remember here is that we are NOT HUMAN!!! Humans enjoy smelling sweet and soapy, but many of us do not. While I actually don't mind baths, many of my friends are terrified of the bath. Since baths can be tortuous for some, your human should ask you what you would like. If you do not enthusiastically take baths, the torture must stop. If, like me, however, you don't mind, or even like, baths, bathing can occur on a schedule that is acceptable to you, not your human. For example, I don't mind the occasional bath, but if they are given too often, my skin gets itchy. For this reason, I have trained my humans to give me a bath every couple of months. I have accomplished this by running away if they try to give me one sooner. Simply running away from them should be enough to teach a human that you are not happy. Due to their innate need to please you, they will hopefully feel guilty for even trying to do something that would make you sad. This guilt should cause them to rethink their ways and stop them from bathing you. If this doesn't work, and sadly some humans are stubborn, simply tremble and cry. They will surely feel guilty and stop their dreadful behavior. A pitiful whimper is also a valuable tool. Humans melt at our whimpers. This technique may even earn you a well-deserved treat as well!

NAIL TRIMS

Nail trims are another grooming practice that humans seem convinced is necessary. Humans believe they are being kind to us by trimming our nails. They believe they are doing what is best for us and saving us from the discomfort of long nails. They are wrong! Many of us are terrified of clippers. And the whole concept of nail trims is terribly confusing to us. Why do humans want to take parts of our nails away from us? We

don't steal their nails! They should not steal ours! While some dogs might not mind the act of getting a mani-pedi, these spa sessions are the bane of a pug's existence. We will do anything to be permitted to embrace our inner sloth and grow our nails long. Once again, your human should ask you what you would like. If you enjoy nail trims, your human can and should make you happy by stealing your nails as often as you'd like. If, like me, you are terrified of the clippers, your humans must stop this crazy behavior.

Training this behavior out of your human is very difficult. The problem seems to be the fact that long nails could potentially curl into our pads and cause us pain when we walk. This is no excuse! However, their need to make us happy makes it difficult for them to see us in pain. Since they honestly believe their behavior is in our best interest, this will take a lot of perseverance on your part. It will also take more than the basic Annoyance or Guilt Methods of training.

Step one of training your human to leave your nails alone is to pull your hands and feet away from them. If they can't hold onto your paw, they can't trim those nails! This rather brilliant technique is often enough to buy you some time. Your human will almost certainly come back with reinforcements, but for a short while your nails will be safe. When reinforcements come, it's time to scream and wail. Embrace your inner banshee! While screaming, it is advisable to flail about to make it more difficult for the humans to hold you. The more you flail, the more dangerous it will become for your human to trim your nails. With dedication, you will win this battle! Sadly, this is a battle that must be fought repeatedly, but eventually your human is sure to abandon all hope of successfully trimming your nails.

FACE WASHING

For some reason, humans like to have clean faces. They wash their faces multiple times a day. As a pug, I can tell you that not all non-humans wish to partake in this practice. Many of us enjoy saving a little food for later on our chins. Others, like us pugs, have wrinkles on our faces. Sometimes these wrinkles get dirty and itchy. Humans seem to see both of these instances as a time for them to "help" us. As you know, we do not need help. We are perfectly capable of cleaning our chins of the scrumptious food. And we are most definitely capable of cleaning our own wrinkles. My usual method is to rub my face on the carpet or furniture, but occasionally the opportunity to rub my face on someone's pillow arises. This is always my favorite way to self-clean.

As with bathing, training this need to wash our faces out of your humans might be difficult. I advise employing the same training methods here. If your human comes to wash your face, run away. If you are trapped, squirm and move your head out of their reach. If they can't hold your head, they can't wash your face! This training method will surely make life difficult for your humans, and humans don't want difficult lives. It will also show your displeasure with their activity. As we learned before, humans have a great need to keep us happy. Expressing your displeasure is sure to make them feel guilty. This guilt will most certainly cause them to stop trying to wash your face. Once again, if this doesn't work, trembling in fear at the sight of the washcloth and whimpering will surely cause them to rethink their ways.

HOUSEHOLD CHORES

As with everything else, humans have some strange ideas about household chores. Specifically, they are constantly doing laundry and vacuuming. These two chores, in particular, are not necessarily something that we appreciate having done. We will need to use a combination of methods to train these behaviors out of our humans.

LAUNDRY DAY

Laundry Day is something humans apparently enjoy. I am of this opinion because Laundry Day happens over and over again. Humans enjoy wearing clean clothes. They like sleeping with "fresh" sheets and blankets. They like to wash everything! Because a happy human is much easier to train, your human should be permitted to have Laundry Day as often as they would like with the stipulation that they only wash their own belongings. This is because we fur babies do not understand the need to wash things.

We understand the world through smell, and it is unfathomable to us that humans do not. We want our world to smell as it should, while humans want everything to smell like flowers or an ocean breeze. And while we enjoy the smell of roses and oceans, we believe that these smells should be limited to their respective objects. When a bed smells like roses, it's confusing. We don't want to sleep on a rosebush. We want to sleep in our bed. And our bed should smell like our bed. As for our toys, we don't want them to smell fresh either. We work very hard to get our toys to smell just right.

Our humans must, therefore, be taught to leave our belongings alone. To teach your human this, we will use the Annoyance Method. Most humans don't like a lot of noise. They find noise annoying. You will therefore make a lot of noise! Cry, bark, and howl when your human takes away your toys and puts them in the washing machine. It may take them a few tries, but eventually your human will learn that your crying means that you are not happy with them. They will learn that when they give your toys a violent bath in the washer, it makes you sad. As we learned earlier, humans do not like it when we are sad. They will surely feel guilty and won't wash your toys the next day. As your humans become better trained, they may even give you a treat for putting up with their bad behavior.

When this happens, it is time for positive reinforcement. You should do this by being helpful. It's time to help them with their laundry. The best way to help them is to sit on top of their laundry pile. First, you will sit on the dirty laundry. They will enjoy trying to get the laundry from under you without disturbing your comfort. Once they are finished washing and drying their clothes, humans enjoy folding everything. If you are lucky, your human will make a pile of clean laundry on the bed or couch. This is where they will fold their clothes. And this is your opportunity to help once again. You will sit on the clean clothes just like you sat of the dirty clothes piles. Your human will once again have the opportunity to pull the laundry out from under you.

Your human will soon learn that Laundry Day isn't the problem. The problem is the washing of your belongings.

VACUUMING

Vacuuming is another activity that humans seem to enjoy, but many of us do not. Humans vacuum often. They will vacuum every room in their house. The problem with this behavior is not the cleanliness, but the terrifying Vacuum Monster that they use to perform this chore. The Vacuum Monster makes a lot of loud noise! And it gobbles things up as it moves along. This can be quite terrifying indeed! This is most definitely a time to use the Guilt Method!

When your humans bring out the Vacuum Monster, it is time for you to run away. Run into the other room as quickly as you can. Hide under the bed if you are able. If you are too big to fit under the bed, jumping onto the bed or couch to escape the monster will work just as well. Once you have found a safe location, it is time to tremble, whimper, and howl. Make sure your human understands how terrified you are. They must be made to understand that there is a very real possibility that you or your toys may be inhaled by the very scary Vacuum Monster that they seem so intent on pushing around your house. Your human must see how truly terrifying this situation is. This will cause them to feel guilty and they will work on ways to minimize your fear while still satisfying their need to interact with the monster.

Eventually your human will learn to leave the Vacuum Monster tucked away in a closet while you are in the room and only bring it out when you are somewhere else. There are many ways in which they may do this. It is up to you to help them choose the method you prefer. They may learn to take you outside to play while they use the monster. Alternatively, they might encourage you to stay in another room because the weather outside isn't to your liking. They might even ask another human to comfort you while they play with their monster. When they find a method that keeps you happy and feeling safe, you must reward them. As with other lessons, positive reinforcement is the best reward. Simply wag your tail and give them kisses. They will be pleased that they have successfully made you feel better and will continue with this behavior.

THE GREAT OUTDOORS

Humans usually enjoy taking us outside. They realize that being outside on a nice day makes us happy. Remember our happiness makes them happy, so training your human to take you outside is quite simple. The problem arises when the weather is not ideal or when you are tired. These situations require additional training.

40

WALKS

Perhaps the easiest lesson to teach your human is to take you on walks. For this lesson, all you need to do is act happy when you realize you are going outside. As soon as your human picks up your leash, begin wagging your tail. You might consider giving your human a happy little hop. This will make them immensely proud because they have successfully made you happy without you having to tell them what you wanted. Remember a happy human is one that is easier to train, so this positive reinforcement is especially important.

CARRIES

You will soon notice that humans are able to walk very quickly. While it usually isn't a problem for larger dogs, those of us who are vertically challenged often have trouble keeping up. It is in these situations that a carry will be useful. The idea of a carry is quite simple. When you are tired, your human should carry you wherever you would like to go.

Training your human to carry you around will once again require the Guilt Method. When you are tired or don't feel like walking, simply find a comfortable place to sit. Sit down and give your human a pitiful look. This pitiful expression of yours will make your human feel sympathetic towards you and extremely guilty for tiring you. Your human will quickly pick you up and carry you the rest of the way. Soon your human will be carrying you everywhere you would like to go.

44

STROLLERS

Strollers are particularly important tools for those of us who are elderly or tire easily and are unable to keep up with our humans. Like a carry, a stroller lets us rest our weary bones while our human gets fresh air. The use of a stroller, however, must be planned at the start of an excursion. The best way to teach your human these planning skills is to repeatedly request a carry. Eventually your human's arms will tire, and they will realize that the simplest solution is to purchase you a stroller. Once the stroller is purchased it is up to them to remember to use it. Since they enjoy being comfortable, they will actually be able to teach themselves to bring your stroller with them. This will be especially pleasant for you because you will be able to enjoy the sights of the outdoors without needing to walk.

INCLEMENT WEATHER

While most of us enjoy the great outdoors, many of us do not enjoy being outside when the weather isn't perfect. Everyone's definition of perfection is different, but to me, if it is not a gorgeous sunny day, I do not want to be outside for very long. I especially do not want to step outside into rainy or snowy weather. Unfortunately, many humans don't understand that their non-human children don't want to be wet. The walk they enjoyed on a sunny day is much less enjoyable on a not so sunny day.

The way to train your human to understand this concept and to behave accordingly is to us the Guilt Method. This method must be used quickly and consistently, or you will most certainly find yourself in a cold and damp situation. When your human wishes to take you outside and you find the conditions less than desirable, it is time to plant your feet. Simply stiffen your legs and refuse to move. This is a good time to add tucking your tail and whining. Your human will be devastated to see that you are not happy and will most certainly change their mind about the dreaded walk in the rain or snow. Sadly, this is a lesson that must be relearned repeatedly by most humans. Remember consistency is key! They will understand and remember eventually.

ABOUT THE AUTHOR

Ginger Block is a 13-year-old pug from Northern Virginia and the author of *So You Found Yourself A Human, Now What? - How To Train Your Human.* After years of teaching humans how to be better pet parents with her weekly Instagram feature, *Scholarly Saturday,* Ginger has now written a book to help non-humans train their human family. It is her greatest desire to see non-humans all over the world enjoy the life they deserve with their well-trained parents.

Ginger enjoys a life of comfort with her humans catering to her every need. Her favorite activities include watching her friends, the neighborhood squirrels, playing in her yard, sleeping in the sun on a beautiful day, sleeping on the couch, and, of course, eating. She enjoys traveling with her family and has visited over 15 states as well as Canada.

You can visit Ginger on Instagram (@GingerBlock).